STIR

CREATION

Stir: Creation ©2018 Cumberland Presbyterian Church, Discipleship Ministry Team

All Rights Reserved. No part of this publication may be reproduced or transmitted in any form or by any means, electronic or mechanical, including photocopying, recording, or by any information storage or retrieval system, without permission in writing from the publisher with the single exception that purchase of this curriculum grants the purchaser the right to copy and distribute student handouts within each lesson for use in their local church. For information address Discipleship Ministry Team, Cumberland Presbyterian Center, 8207 Traditional Place, Cordova (Memphis), Tennessee, 38016-7414.

Funded, in part, by your contributions to Our United Outreach.

Published by The Discipleship Ministry Team, CPC
Memphis, Tennessee

Layout and Design by Tandem Creative Company, LLC.
Some wave, mountain and tree imagery taken from Creativetoons-Freepik.com and Kjpargeter-Freepik.com.

ISBN-13: 978-1-945929-15-1
ISBN-10: 1-945929-15-4

STIR

TABLE OF CONTENTS

INTRODUCTION 1

SUGGESTED USES 2

LESSON 1: GOOD

    HEAD SECTION 3

    HEART SECTION 5

    HAND SECTION 7

LESSON 2: BROKEN

    HEAD SECTION 8

    HEART SECTION 10

    HAND SECTION 12

LESSON 3: REDEEMED

    HEAD SECTION 13

    HEART SECTION 17

    HAND SECTION 18

INTRODUCTION

Back in 2015, I spent time speaking with youth workers and asking them about curriculum. One of the main things I took from those conversations was that most youth workers weren't using curriculum in the same manner as it is still being written. Many youth workers that I talked with expressed how they would pick and choose elements to use as a part of their talks or lessons. They weren't looking for "paint by numbers" resources, but rather things that would help them stir the faith imaginations of the students they lead. With those conversations in mind and with the help and creativity of many different pastors, youth workers, and teachers, we dreamed of a resource that could be used as a standard curriculum, but also function in a way that youth leaders of today need. Stir is our response to that need. Our hope is that it will help youth workers create resources that will supplement the good work they are doing and stir the faith imaginations of their students.

The theme for our first Stir is *creation*. God's creation and our role within God's creation is a big topic. Our hope is that using Stir will give you the tools you need to inspire young people to be in awe of God's creation, see our role in its brokenness, and be moved to come alongside God as partners in the redemption of God's beautiful creation.

The curriculum is broken into 3 lessons, focusing on God's *Good, Broken,* and *Redeemed* creation. Within each lesson are three parts: Head, Heart, and Hands. Head represents a teaching about that specific lesson. For instance, there may be scripture discussion, a sermon outline, talking points, a lesson video, etc. Heart will be the creative or evocative portion that may have a lesson video, liturgy, song reflection, etc. Hands will be activities or ways that your group can move toward action.

Stir can be used as small group lessons, theme and material for retreats or camps, or part of a sermon series, but one of the main goals is to give you lots of unique and helpful tools so you can incorporate them into discussion with your group about God's creation. We can't wait to hear about all the ways you use Stir and how it helps to stir your group's faith imagination.

Peace,
Nathan

SUGGESTED USES

We want you to be able to use this resource in a multitude of ways so here are a few ideas for you to see the different ways to use *Stir: Creation* in different settings. These outlines are created from elements in Lesson 1 from *Stir: Creation*.

SMALL GROUP OUTLINE

Welcome
Intro for Lesson
Read Genesis 1
Use Talking Points (focused on Genesis 1:2-4)
Teaching Video
Discussion
Take Home: Photography Project

LARGE GROUP OUTLINE

Welcome/Announcements
Liturgy
Songs
Teaching Video or Sermon (on Genesis 1)
Activity: Photography Project
Song
Prayer

RETREAT / CAMP SMALL GROUP OUTLINE

Welcome
Read Genesis 1
Talking Points (focused on Genesis 1:2-4)
Quiet time (taking note of God's good creation)
Small Group Sharing
Prayer

RETREAT / CAMP WORSHIP OUTLINE

Liturgy
Songs
Teaching Video
Sermon Outline (Genesis 1)
Song
Quiet time

LESSON 1: GOOD
Scripture Passage: Genesis 1

INTRODUCTION

The first lesson of *Stir: Creation* is on God's good creation. Most of the resources in this lesson focus on Genesis 1. It's one of the creation stories in Genesis (Genesis 2 being the other). Genesis 1 tells how and what God created and that God's original creation was good. In this lesson there is a sermon outline, a teaching video, talking points, a liturgy, and some activities for you to use to create a lesson centering on God's good creation.

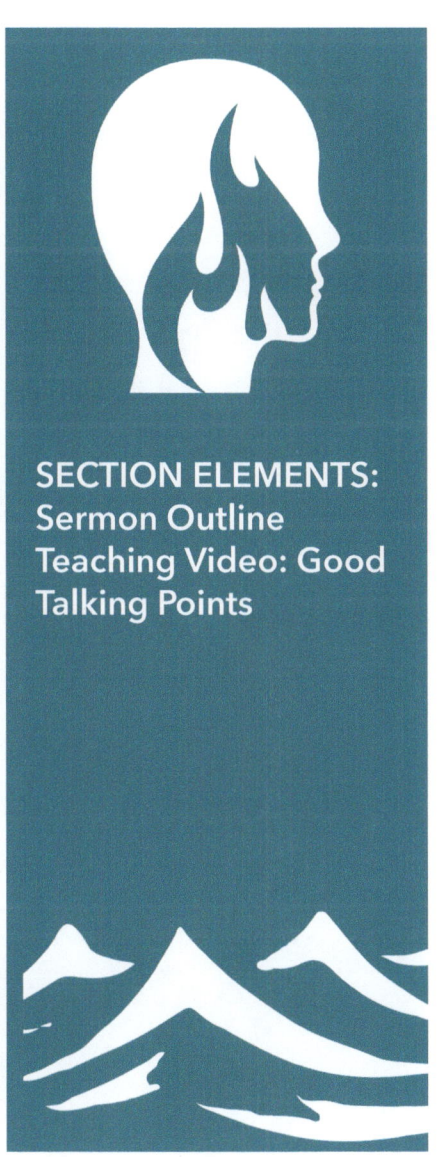

SECTION ELEMENTS:
Sermon Outline
Teaching Video: Good
Talking Points

SERMON / TALK OUTLINE

This outline is to help you craft a sermon / talk using Genesis 1. You can use these bullet points as a jumping off point to help you as you begin to develop a talk/sermon about Genesis 1.

- We understand that God's goodness is present at all times.

- How often do we consider that God's goodness is present in all places and settings?

- Still creating

- Wonder and awe at the creativity
    Big – vastness of oceans and mountains; solar systems; ecosystems
    Small – intricacies of the bigger systems
    Variety – diversity and unity existing in the world

- People are a part of God's good creation, participating as part of the good of creation

TEACHING VIDEO: GOOD

This video was created as a way to help your group connect to the good of God's creation. Due to all the bad we see, it's often difficult to focus on the good. This video could be used as the lesson for an evening service or maybe as an introduction to your discussion and/or a talk in your group.

https://cpcmc.org/stir

SCRIPTURE GUIDE: GENESIS 1:2-4

These talking points are to help either in a discussion of Genesis 1:2-4 or to be a guide as you craft a lesson on that scripture.

1. Things to consider in this scripture: the goodness of each created thing, God's creativity, and how we belong to God's creation.

2. We often say that God is good all the time. What about God being good in all places and in all created things?

3. These verses tell a story of how God has made all things, but is creation a one-time occurrence? How is God continuously creating?

4. Consider the wonders of the created world – both its vastness and its intricacies, and consider the creativity and artistry of God's handiwork.

5. Through the course of each day, God declares that the creation is good or very good. What does it mean that all the created things are good?

6. People are the last ones on the scenes of this creation story. What role do these people play in the story? What role do we play in the goodness of God's creativity?

SECTION ELEMENTS:
Liturgy
Video: Noah
Stills

LITURGY

This liturgy is written as a call and responsive prayer that can be used during a worship setting for a retreat or to open a Sunday school lesson about God's good creation.

Regular text: Leader; **Bold** text: All

In the beginning,
God created.
Light.
Air.
And the waters gathered,
and created land.
And the lights took their places,
and created seasons, time, tides, growth.
And the waters and the air
brought forth creatures.
And the land
brought forth creatures.
And together God said,
"Let us make something in our image."
And together, humankind was entrusted
and blessed with all that was made.
God said then, and says now, "It's your turn."

So we begin.
In the beginning, we create.
Light into darkness.
Space to breathe.
Some days we say,
"It is good."
And some days we do not.
But each day we begin again.
We gather.
We take our place.
We foster life.
We are co-creators.
God says it is good.
It is good.

VIDEO: NOAH

There are many movies that depict God's creation, but one you may want to show comes from the 2014 Russell Crowe movie *Noah*. One part of the film has Noah explaining the creation story to his kids while they are gathered in the Ark. Below is a YouTube link for that movie clip.

www.youtube.com/watch?v=OwSWRdbSQK0

SECTION ELEMENTS:
Photography Project
Additional Activities

PHOTOGRAPHY PROJECT

A way to connect to God's good creation is to be aware that it surrounds us. We need to pay attention to how God speaks to us through the beauty and awe of creation. This week take time to notice God's good creation. Encourage this awareness by having your group participate in a photography project.

CHALLENGE: Have your group create a crowdsource online collage. **Crowdsource** *means to create something using a large group of people.*

1. Any time you notice God's good creation, take a picture using your phone or tablet.

2. Post that picture on Instagram or Twitter using the hashtag #stircreationgood

3. Along with their post, encourage your group to share what feelings or thoughts God stirred in them.

4. These pictures will then be searchable using that hashtag and you can see how your group is connecting to God's good creation that week.

ADDITIONAL ACTIVITIES

Another good way to help your group think about God's good creation is using food! Ask someone in your congregation or community who gardens to share why they do and how it connects with God's good creation. Another way is to prepare a meal using only locally produced food. You may want to take a field trip to visit a farm or go to a local famer's market and speak to people about why they decided to grow their own food.

LESSON 2: BROKEN
Scripture Passage: Genesis 3

INTRODUCTION

This lesson focuses on the brokenness of God's good creation. In Genesis 3, we read about humanity's break from God's good design and the consequences of that. In this lesson is a teaching video, talking points on Genesis 3, scripture discussion questions, suggested videos and activities you can use to craft a lesson about God's broken creation.

SECTION ELEMENTS:
Teaching Video:
Broken
Talking Points
Scripture Discussion

TEACHING VIDEO

We created this video as a way to tell the story of Genesis 3 in a fresh and evocative way. It's a story that has been heard many times and has many points. This video helps to tie Genesis 3 into a larger story of sin and its role in the brokenness of all of God's creation.

https://cpcmc.org/stir

TALKING POINTS: GENESIS 3

These talking points are to help either in discussion of Genesis 3 or to be a guide as you craft a lesson on that scripture.

1. Things to consider in this scripture: Humans choosing to be separate/above rather than a part of creation; how something good can become tainted; hiding from God; consequences for their actions.

2. Why do you think God asked Adam and Eve not to eat from the tree in the middle of the garden?

3. You've probably heard someone observe that when someone tells you not to do something it makes you want to do that thing even more. With that being said, do you think God was wrong to tell Eve and Adam not to eat from the tree because God knew they would do it anyway?

TALKING POINTS: GENESIS 3 *continued*

4. What do you think about the serpent? Do you think the serpent knew what would happen? If so, why would it risk its own well being?

5. Why do you think Adam and Eve thought they could hide from God? What do you try to hide from God?

6. What choices do you see others making that lead to the brokenness of creation? What choices have you made that separate you from creation?

SCRIPTURE DISCUSSION QUESTIONS: ROMANS 8:18-25

This scripture from Romans speaks of God's broken creation. In the scripture it talks about how all of creation groans for redemption from the brokenness created by sin. Here are some questions to ask after reading this passage.

1. In what ways do we see the world suffering?

2. What are we and the earth longing for?

3. We mourn with creation/alongside creation.

4. Freedom from what?

5. We (all of creation, not just people) were saved. Saved from what for what?

SECTION ELEMENTS:
Videos
Documentaries
Stills
Song

VIDEOS

Below are some suggested videos that you can use as you create your lesson on God's broken creation. The first video was created around a song by Silver Mt. Zion. I first heard this song covered by the band The Gentle Wolves who used it as a part of a service of lament. The lyrics for the song are "when the world is sick, can't no one be well, but I dreamt we was all beautiful and strong." Maybe this could be used as an opening to a talk, sermon or perhaps as a reflective piece afterwards.

vimeo.com/14827280

The second video was suggested in Lesson 1 but it may very well work here. This is from the movie *Noah* starring Russel Crowe as Noah. In this clip Noah is explaining to his family the story of creation and it ends with the consequences now upon them for the choices made by humanity.

www.youtube.com/watch?v=OwSWRdbSQK0

The third video is a scene from *Sesame Street* where Oscar is taught the word for trash in Spanish "Basura."

www.youtube.com/watch?v=6b8iumcxf4E

DOCUMENTARIES

There are a number of documentaries that might be a good way to share the severity of the brokenness of creation. Maybe you could show one of these during a retreat or camp or as a part of the series of God's creation. Below is an blog from UPROXX that has 7 suggested documentaries that might be good to use.

uproxx.com/life/documentary-environmental-climate-change-earth/8/

SONG

Several years ago I attended a show at Lipscomb University called Tokens. It was set up as an old time radio program and the theme for the night was creation. During that show, there was a young man named Nathan Hale who had written a song called *Infinite Energy* using the insight and words of Wendell Berry. It's a beautiful song that shares the idea of the absurdity of "throwing something away." Nathan agreed to let use his song for this lesson. The words and chords for the song are below. This song may be a great song to share during your retreat or camp or as a theme song for your study on God's creation. Here is a video of his performance that night at Tokens:

www.youtube.com/watch?v=3mhN3Sjy0oU

Infinite Energy by Nate Hale
Capo on 4

```
   C      G       D Em C
I discovered infinity today
   G                  D Em
it wasn't very big at all...
 C  G    D  Em
I was reading Berry
     C      G         D Em
and all blindness turned to day
       C    G                   D Em
in the midst of all the things he had to say
        C    G    D...
he said that it isn't infinite...    if it can't be destroyed.
```

he said that every *living* thing
uses the same currency
water, dirt, and light
and energy is never lost this way
it's just simply changing forms
it's just food for the next thing
and it goes spinning on and on
and at the end of the day
money isn't worth a thing
because you can't eat a dollar bill

```
   G     D     Em     C
yet I buy and use and throw away
    G     D        Em C
and then it's all sold back to me
   G    D    Em    C
I chase this paper economy
   G   D       Em    C
I live a life with broken ends
   G    D             Em      C
I have to bend them back around again
     G    D   Em    C
and mend this broken circle I'm in
```

he said, machines don't work this way
they move in lines from use to waste
there is no creature to change its form
so waste it will remain
it neither lives nor dies nor decays
I am a living breathing thing
but I live the life of a machine

I buy and use and throw away
I break the cycle once again
I chase this paper economy
So I can buy it all again
I live a life with broken ends
I have to mend this broken circle I'm in

SECTION ELEMENTS:
Tracing Your Carbon Footprint
How Far Does Your Food Travel?
Is It Trash?

TRACING YOUR CARBON FOOTPRINT

We know that humanity has played a hand in the brokenness of God's creation. There are many ways that we can begin the work of realizing that impact. One way is calculating your carbon footprint. Carbon Footprint is defined as the amount of carbon dioxide and other carbon compounds emitted due to the consumption of fossil fuels by a particular person, group, etc. Below is a link to a resource that you can use to help your group calculate your carbon footprint individually or as a group.

www.conservation.org/act/carboncalculator/calculate-your-carbon-footprint.aspx#/

HOW FAR DOES YOUR FOOD TRAVEL?

One of the ways people are trying to help reduce their impact on creation is to think about food and where and how far their food travels to get to their plate. We know that the further it travels the more energy and fuel is needed which leads to more pollution. Here is a helpful PDF that speaks about food travel in the Chicago area. It also has additional links to more about food travel in the United States.

ucanr.edu/datastoreFiles/608-319.pdf

IS IT TRASH?

Supplies needed for this activity: Trash bags, gloves, bins, white board

Send your group to collect litter they find around your church, on the side of the road, or maybe at a local park. Divide the group into small groups or go as individuals to pick up the trash.

Gather the group together. Have bins designated for recycling and for trash. Work together to determine if the items you picked up are recyclable or actual trash. Keep a tally of the number of items that were waste and those that could be recycled. After you have designated items to recycle, look at all the waste items. As a group consider how this waste could have been prevented. Also invite the group to think of some way to make use of the waste. (Some food waste can be composted; some materials can be washed to be used; you may be able to use materials for artwork. Let your imaginations run wild!)

STIR Curriculum - Lesson 2: Broken

LESSON 3: REDEEMED
Scripture Passage: Exodus 20:8

INTRODUCTION

This third lesson is designed to help your group think about how we can be a part of God's redeemed creation. God is at work in us and through us to redeem what is broken. In this lesson there is a devotional on Sabbath, a spoken word or responsive reading, a video liturgy, and some activities for you to use to build a lesson on God's redeemed creation.

SECTION ELEMENTS:
Devotion
Spoken Word / Responsive Reading

DEVOTION

This devotion was written to help us think about how keeping the Sabbath is connected to the redemption of all of God's good and broken creation. In Exodus 20 God speaks the ten commandments. In verse 8, we read that we are to remember and keep the Sabbath holy. This devotion is a reflection on Sabbath keeping. This could be read aloud, printed in a devotion book at your retreat or camp or shared during a Sunday school lesson.

Exodus 20:8 "Remember the Sabbath day by keeping it holy." (NIV)

What is Sabbath? In scripture, we read that it is a command to keep a day holy. The Hebrew word "Shabbat" means to rest or cease.

When is the last day you rested? I don't mean binge watching Netflix or hibernating all day. I mean set a day aside to rest. I would venture to say it's hard to remember doing that. Say you have though, how many of us can say that not only have we set aside a day for rest but set aside a day to have holy rest? That's the command of Sabbath.

The command reads remember the Sabbath day by keeping it holy. Let's look at that for a minute. What are we to remember specifically?

> *Six days you shall labor and do all your work, but the seventh day is a sabbath to the Lord your God. On it you shall not do any work, neither you, nor your son or daughter, nor your male or female servant, nor your animals, nor any foreigner residing in your towns. For in six days the Lord made the heavens and the earth, the sea, and all that is in them, but he rested on the seventh day. Therefore the Lord blessed the Sabbath day and made it holy.* Exodus 20:9-11 (NIV)

13 STIR Curriculum - Lesson 3: Redeemed

In Deuteronomy, we are to remember that "you were slaves in Egypt and that the Lord your God brought you out…" So we are to remember to practice Sabbath because God freed people from their bondage in Egypt.

When the commandment teaches us to "remember" it is a two-fold remembrance. To remember God's hand in the creation of the world and everyone in it and God's mighty and outstretched arm to an enslaved people.

The command says to remember by keeping it holy. So we've got the remember part but what is the holy part?

In Exodus, it is because God created and then rested that the Sabbath is holy. It was the rhythmic act of creating and resting. In Deuteronomy it doesn't say that it is holy but rather we should observe it because the Lord God commanded us to. I want to take these two parts and make one whole observation when it comes to keeping the Sabbath. To practice Sabbath is to practice holy rest and I use that word "practice" literally.

We are to practice the holy rhythm God instilled into the very molecules used to create the world and all that is in it. To labor and rest. To remember and act.

To labor, create, and work is a part of life. But it is not the whole of our lives. God helps us remember that once people were slaves, forced under brutal conditions to work without rest, without ceasing. To rest is a reminder that we were created by a beloved God. To remember that rest is not laziness but holy rest is in fact holy. To rest is to do an action that reflects the desire of God for the world and all that is in it to have a day of rest.

I believe that God doesn't want us to lie around all day, or do nothing at all on our day of Sabbath. I think the type of Sabbath keeping God commands is one that allows all of us to experience a day of rest. Six days where we work towards living a life where all can experience one day of holy rest together. It's the redemption of us and God's creation.

I feel like for a lot of my life, the Sabbath was explained in a way that felt almost like a day to be selfish instead of selfless.

One Sabbath Jesus was going through the grainfields, and as his disciples walked along, they began to pick some heads of grain. The Pharisees said to him, "Look, why are they doing what is unlawful on the Sabbath?" He answered, "Have you never read what David did when he and his companions were hungry and in need? In the days of Abiathar the high priest, he entered the house of God and ate the consecrated bread, which is lawful only for priests to eat. And he also gave some to his companions." Then [Jesus] said to them, "The Sabbath was made for man, not man for the Sabbath. So the Son of Man is Lord even of the Sabbath." Mark 2:23-28 (NIV)

Being selfless, thinking of others, caring for someone in need is not just a part of Sabbath keeping, it is Sabbath. It's a day we can come alongside God to redeem creation. Holy rest places itself in the act of rest and ceasing. Resting in the love of God, and stopping or ceasing action that would deny rest for others.

Sabbath was made for men.

Sabbath was made for women.

Sabbath was made for children.

Sabbath was made for us and them.

Sabbath was made for the animals of all kinds and the world in which we both live.

Sabbath was made to redeem all of God's creation.

SPOKEN WORD / RESPONSIVE READING

This reflection focuses on where the way of Christ leads us. It could be used as part of a worship service centered on God's redeemed creation or as a responsive reading or liturgical prayer.

The story goes that God looks out into chaos and sends Wind to create. Divine Breath brushes dirt and in God's image we begin. One with the Spirit.

Chaos still lurking, we're given boundaries for our safety and prosperity and wholeness. Love says, "It's better to stay." Yet, Love also sets us free.

We explore the beauty, the wonder of creation. We see the boundaries, we remember Love's words, but we put Trust to the test. We walk out on Love. Our bond with Perfect is broken.

Faithfulness remains steadfast in guidance as we wander. Sometimes, we approach Home. Sometimes, we run as far as our legs will take us in the opposite direction. Sometimes, we just don't move. Love, though abandoned, stays near. This unfathomable, patient, Grace.

God does not forget. Always creating, always loving, always breathing Life.

Life – into the body of the least of these – a baby to a sojourning, unwed family. A child born into turmoil, the chaos we have chosen – the broken systems we endorse – the division we perpetuate. Yet Grace comes to show us the Way.

And He grows. And He sees and hears and learns. He is ever-close to Home, never abandoning Love, walking the path set by Faithfulness, One with the Spirit. Eternally bonded to Perfect.

He is Hope. Our Hope. That God would send this One, human, dirt brushed with Divine Breath - just as we were - and yet also Perfect. He remembers the way Home. Hope will lead us there. Grace shows the Way.

He teaches. He lives. He moves and acts and works. He speaks. All among the chaos. Right there in the thick of it. Deep in the mess, he makes the Way.

We hesitate. Where once we chose the chaos, now we want the beauty. Could he not take a different way? Take us through gardens. Take us by still waters. Take us safely around the mess. It's too ugly, too damaged, too broken here. Take another way, we plead. We want another way. We imagine another way.

We build other ways. Promises, prosperity, safety, pretty places to read pretty books while dressed in pretty clothes - they sound like the better way. Idols.

The Way has been marked in the dirt. A line in the sand. The garden is stained with tears. The waters are not still, they pour with blood from His side. The Way is not safe. It must go through the brokenness, the chaos we have chosen. Love still with us, Hope ahead, Peace, working to keep the path clear.

The Christ. From birth to death he was showing the Way. Like Wind, we are sent into the chaos to create - Love, Faith, Hope, Peace are our helpmates. Co-creators with God we enter the chaos. Following Christ, we wade in the depths of the mess. We are called to teach and live and move and act and work and speak in ways that shape this chaotic, broken, divided space into a place where Righteousness, Justice, Freedom, and Joy reside.

We know this is the work we must do. We know this is how we must live. We are sure that this Way through the mess is where it is better to stay because our story doesn't end in death but in Life.

Division, brokenness, and chaos do not win. They lead to death. They crucify Hope. But they do not have the last word.

Reconciliation. Restoration. Renewal. This is where the Way leads, and until this world looks more like Home, we work to rebuild, because Grace has shown us the way.

SECTION ELEMENTS:
Visual Liturgy Video
Stills

VISUAL LITURGY VIDEO

This video is a reflection on Psalm 8:3-9 & Psalm 24:1-6. It incorporates some phrases and images from those scriptures. This video could be used as a visual liturgy for your group or as the opening video to a worship gathering.

https://cpcmc.org/stir

SECTION ELEMENTS:
Sleeping Mat
Trash Art

SLEEPING MATS

One way we can help in redeeming God's creation is taking something and creating a new use for it. Plastic bags are known to be a hazard to God's creation but many people are turning plastic bags into a sleeping mat for those who are experiencing homelessness. Take a look at this article online about plastic bag sleeping mats.

thesavvyage.com/turn-your-plastic-bags-into-sleeping-mats/

This could be an ongoing project for your group to collect the bags and create some mats!

TRASH ART

Take the trash that you collected from Lesson 2 and have folks come up with ways they can redeem this garbage. Create a piece of art, or restore it so it can be useful again. Have groups brainstorm ways to redeem the collected garbage and have them do it!

RESOURCES

BOOKS

Ekblad, Bob. **Reading the Bible with the Damned.** Louisville: Westminster John Knox Press, 2005.
Fretheim, Terence E. "The Book of Genesis." Keck, Leander E. **The New Interpreters Bible.** Nashville: Abingdon Press, 1994.
Von Rad, Gerhard. **Genesis.** Philadelphia: The Westminster Press, 1972.

WEBSITES

YouTube
 www.youtube.com/watch?v=OwSWRdbSQK0
 www.youtube.com/watch?v=6b8iumcxf4E
 www.youtube.com/watch?v=3mhN3Sjy0oU

Vimeo.com
 vimeo.com/14827280

Uproxx.com
 uproxx.com/life/documentary-environmental-climate-change-earth/8/

Conservation.org
 www.conservation.org/act/carboncalculator/calculate-your-carbon-footprint.aspx#/

Uncanr.edu
 ucanr.edu/datastoreFiles/608-319.pdf

Thesavvyage.com
 thesavvyage.com/turn-your-plastic-bags-into-sleeping-mats/

MUSIC

Infinite Energy song written and performed by Nathan Hale, inspired by selected readings of Wendell Berry. For more music by Nate go to natehale.bandcamp.com/

ADDITIONAL RESOURCES USED IN *STIR* CREATION

theworkofthepeople.com
Textweek.com
Biblegateway.com
Noah by Darren Aronofsky
God Bless our Dead Marines by Silver Mt. Zion
When the World Is Sick (refrain from God Bless our Dead Marines by Silver Mt. Zion) covered by The Gentle Wolves
Readings of Wendell Berry
CEB, NIV, NRSV Bible translations
To find more info, including stills and videos go to https://cpcmc.org/stir.

SPECIAL THANKS TO...

Tandem Creative Company, Hannah Pahl, Anna Brockman, Marcus Hayes, Whitney Brown and BJ Mathis for your creativity, wisdom, and collaboration that helped to make *Stir: Creation*.

NOTES:

NOTES:

NOTES:

NOTES:

NOTES:

NOTES:

NOTES:

www.ingramcontent.com/pod-product-compliance
Lightning Source LLC
Chambersburg PA
CBHW060802090426
42736CB00002B/125